Lessons for Economies in Transition

The Case of Elgeyo Marakwet County (EMC), Kenya

By Paul Kipchumba

Designed and Published by:
Kipchumba Foundation
P.O. Box 25380 – 00100 Nairobi, Kenya
www.kipchumbafound.org

©
2019
Paul Kipchumba
This book is intended to serve as website and social media material for *Elgeyo Marakwet County (EMC), Kenya, Agenda* conversations.

Acknowledgement

I would like to recognize the efforts of every one of the Elgeyo Marakwet residents and their friends on the social media for shaping my ideas about the local conditions in fundamental ways. I had very intense conversations that enabled me to think further and also to come up with more in-depth understanding of the local situation. It's my hope that this collection of my daily reports from December 2018 through January 2019 will be useful in expanding the place of progressive discourse in local development. Specifically, I would like to recognize the administrators of the *EMC Agenda: SWOT Analysis* Whatsapp group Theophilus Ayabei, Titus K. Suter, Janet Kiyeng, and Peter Cheboi for enabling controlled discussions. In addition, I recognize the efforts of Cosmas Rutto Cheptoo Lotirghor and Allan Kiprop Mereng for making bold and consistent submissions for discussion. Finally, I repay special debt of gratitude to the administrators and members of Maraqwet Qlobally Facebook group who consistently published my daily reports and also engaged me in breakthrough conversations.

Content

Introduction..7

Abbreviations and Acronyms...9

Key Names..11

A Blueprint for a Lost Decade, 2013-2022............................12

Switch from Grains (Maize) to Fruits (Avocado) Is Bankruptcy of Economic Ideas..15

Little Emphasis on Qualified Employees by County Public Service Board (CPSB)...17

Leader of Senate Majority Position is a Scam.......................18

EMC Does Not Exercise Power at the National Government...19

Mango Factory is the Worst Industrial Attempt....................20

EMC Propaganda Economy..22

Agriculture Can Never Be the Backbone of Future EMC Economy, Tourism Should Be..23

EMC Semi-Pastoral Economy. Is There Anything to Write Home?..24

EMC Still a County of Champions?...................................25

Why Tolgos Will Get into Even More Trouble Soon...............27

Gorillas in Rimoi Park..29

Land Demarcation Will Make EMC Poorer.........................30

EMC Witness to Transformation......................................31

The Future of Business is Small Business...........................32

Mega Developments as Community Investments..................33

Rise of Female Politicians a Sign of EMC Transformation.......34

Still a Long Way to Universal Access to Safe, Clean (Drinking) Water in EMC..35

Policy Miracles Needed to Make Some Progress on the EMC Integrated Development Plan (CIDP), 2018-2022...................36

EMC Government Should Apologize for Misleading Sections of CIDP, 2018-2022..37

Pre-School and Vocational Education Can Transform EMC.....39

There is Limited Commercialization of Forest Resources in the EMC CIDP, 2018-2022..40

Energy and Mineral Resources Should Not Be a Major Concentration of EMC..41

Agriculture Component of County Integrated Development Plan (CIDP), 2018-2022...42

EMC CIDP, 2018-2022, Is an Additional Challenge on the Challenges of CIDP, 2013-2017...43

Suspicion about Ghost Workers in EMC Can Be Cured by Technological Verification..44

Alleviating Every Challenge in EMC by Industrialization and Urbanization...45

Is Artificial Intelligence (AI) a Threat?..46

Tearing Apart Prevailing Amorphous Sense of Status Quo in EMC Will Create Room for the Rise of the Rest....................48

EMC Blame Game in Resolving Cattle Rustling...................49

Anti-FGM Struggles Are of No Direct Economic Benefit to EMC...50

Resolving Low Productivity in EMC...................................51

EMC Needs Credible Economic Statistics...........................52

Regulation, Modernization, and Promotion of *Chang'aa* and *Busaa* Is the Way to Go for EMC..53

Let's Develop Our Cooperatives...55

EMC Formalities versus Development....................................56

Get Out, Get Down to Work..57

Establishing a "No Weapons Corridor" at Border Areas..........58

Let's Move Our People to Commercial Centres Where We Can Provide Them with Modern Services.....................................59

A Mini Library in Every Ward in EMC..................................60

Poverty Eradication Should Be the Rallying Agenda in EMC....61

Let's Sue the Government in 2019 over Compensation for Cattle Rustling Losses...62

Cable Cars without a Vibrant Tourism Economy Is Wrong......63

Developing a Tourist Attraction or an Equivalent Industrial System in Every Ward..64

Overconcentration on EMC Government Is Small Thinking.....65

The Idea of Building Museums in EMC Is Welcome but with Caution..66

Missing Details of Modern Industry in EMC.........................67

Myths of Youth Unemployment in EMC...............................68

Time for an Industrial EDA..69

Shedding Tears for a Lost Proposed Kerio University.............70

Annex: Elgeyo Marakwet Councillors, 1925-1963....................71

Introduction

Between the beginning of December 2018 and mid-January 2019 I spent most of my time interacting and conversing with, mostly, residents of Elgeyo Marakwet County in Kenya, where I was born and brought up. I tried to engage at least 40,000 of them every day on the social media by making short but informed submissions about pertinent issues concerning them and their county government. That attempt was my way of coming to terms with the realities of what undermines development in most developing economies, especially in Africa.

I premised the whole idea on a book form that has the potential for continuous additions, corrections and tracking on a MediaWiki website and social media platforms. I drafted an outline of the book and some rules for guiding the process. When I was compiling this work, the writing process was on course towards engagement of the local communities through Short Text Messages (SMS) with the support of FrontlineSMS communications management platform.

As you can read from my daily reporting here, including the piece of advice that I extended to the young people "Get Out, Get Down to Work" ((Supplementary Reporting: Friday 04 January 2019), some of the key takeaways that have left some imprint in my mind include veering off issue-based discussions to about-the-individual life and character assessment. My life, especially religious underpinnings, marital status, contributions to local fundraisings (*harambee*), and relationship with the Chinese, formed a significant part of the discussions. I was hard put to respond to all the questions asked. With respect to being unmarried, I replied that I was on course to getting married in 2019 and that I preferred fewer number of children, perhaps only one. This Chinese fashion of one-child policy did not go down well with most of the members of the audience. Some thought that I was *de-indigenoused* and an adopted Chinese, whereas others were of the view that I feared responsibility.

But the most heated discussions were on my lack of direct contribution to local fundraisings (*harambee*). While some of the pundits were convinced that I made some charity contributions to the local communities through Kipchumba Foundation, they held some reservations about my lack of contributions in such social functions because it was seen as more of a cultural challenge than of a deficiency of generosity. I explained to them that at the outset of independence in 1963, Kenya was at the same level of economic development with South Korea. South Korea directed her people to rigorous work and improved productivity, whereas Kenya adopted African socialism (*harambee*) that directed her people to handouts and political cronyism, which I observed in one of my social media engagements under sycophancy as entirely unAfrican.

The second issue that was even more telling was my discussion of advanced technology, especially Artificial Intelligence (AI). Some of the members of the social media group left one of the groups, terming me anti-Christ. It was a similar experience when I introduced FrontlineSMS open source software that has the intelligent capacity to receive, sort, reply, and forward tens of thousands of Short Text Message (SMS) at instant. In one of my reports I indicated that fear of technology is a swipe card to poverty and backwardness.

Finally, the concept of government was shrouded in serious mysteries. Whereas the limitations of the county government were not clear, equally the expectations of the citizens were not clear. It left a big gap that was nearly impossible to bridge by any meaningful consensus. I joined the debates when most of the residents were of the view that they were on course to losing a decade of development in the period 2013-2022 because of poor governance. I tried as much as possible to offer some alternative perspectives, but it was not that easy because very many political and underhand tactics were peddled to undermine the course of the process. Then I concluded that a culture-wide philosophy towards work and common progress was missing, making the residents to focus on one another, not on development.

Paul Kipchumba
Kapenguria, West Pokot County, Kenya
January 2019

Abbreviations and Acronyms

AI:	Artificial Intelligence/ Artificial Insemination
AIC:	African Inland Church
ADC:	African District Council
CCTV:	Closed Circuit Television
CIDP:	County Integrated Development Plan
CPSB:	County Public Service Board
DC:	District Commissioner
ECDE:	Early Childhood Development and Education
EDA:	Equitable Development Act, 2015
EMC:	Elgeyo Marakwet County
EMCian:	A resident of Elgeyo Marakwet County
FDI:	Foreign Direct Investment
FGM:	Female Genital Mutilation/ female circumcision
HDI:	Human Development Index
HIV/ AIDS:	Human Immunodeficiency Virus/ Acquired Immunodeficiency Syndrome
IFMIS:	Integrated financial Management Information System
IGA:	Income Generating Activity
KES:	Kenya Shillings
KVDA:	Kerio Valley Development Authority
LNC:	Local Native Council

NPS:	National Police Service
PSC:	Public Service Commission
TVET:	Technical and Vocational Education and Training
UN:	United Nations
Whatsapp:	A social media platform

Key Names

Marakwet: Ethno-linguistic community in Elgeyo Marakwet County

Pokot: Ethno-linguistic community in Baringo and West Pokot counties

Tolgos: Alex Tanui Tolgos, the Governor Elgeyo Marakwet County (EMC), 2013-present

A Blueprint for a Lost Decade, 2013-2022

Monday 03 January 2019

Recently I have taken interest in the affairs of Elgeyo Marakwet County, not for personal economic interests because after all I am a casualty of poor leadership at the county, but because a young man from the county asked me why I was not employed by the county government. I replied that I have not tendered my name for employment and that there are very many young people who are smarter than I who are interested and can develop the county perfectly well, given the chance. He retorted, "There is no room for a smart person at the county, unless the smart person is related to the governor or his surrogates, and that the smart person is ready and willing to draw salary without work or arrange for kickbacks from contractors and suppliers on behalf of the governor and his men!"

I was shocked.

Then I decided to link up with one of the county bureaucrats, with an aim of contributing to the culture and tourism component, which is part of my ongoing work among the EMC communities, especially in the Kerio Valley. The bureaucrat replied to me that the county cannot employ people as confused as I am. Although I excused him for that unfortunate attitude by keeping off, when I reflected on it later, I thought that we have installed a rogue regime at the county.

That remark energized my resolve into delving deeper into the statecraft of our county. I began checking the attitudes of the bureaucrats and proceedings of the County Assembly. I was shocked again that up to this stage of devolution the benefits of the county system of governance have not trickled down to the local people. In fact, the economic condition for most residents of the county is worse than before the advent of devolution.

The proceedings at the County Assembly are not pro-development at all. They are not strategic. They are not geared towards curbing nepotism, corruption, inefficiency, or creating jobs for the young people. There is no written evidence of industrial progress or intention at all. Equally, there is no evidence of any other related progressive schemes that the young people would expect and/ or envision.

In addition, the executive arm of the county government has not managed to tap talent because the smarter young people have concluded that the county government of Elgeyo Marakwet is a network of nepotism - in most of the social media reports I have studied, the young people call it *a county of tilyanty* (in simple form: *tilyantism*). For the smarter men and women working at the county, they have been placed under below average bosses, some of whom with questionable intellectual capabilities. This has led to demoralized staff, low productivity and general indifference to pursuit of common county interest.

In the process, I decided to begin doing a collective book program, where I am the leader. The title is *Lessons for Economies in Transition: Elgeyo Marakwet County, Kenya*. And my writing this article was to enlist as many young people as possible into the book project that was intended to serve as a classic case for governance and economic development in developing economies by reflecting on Elgeyo Marakwet County, Kenya, into the distant future by making bold practical economic and philosophical suggestions.

The first objective was to critically examine the proceedings of the County Assembly, the past county projects, and human resources and their working relationships. I observed that there was a higher likelihood of incriminating evidence against the governor and other staff at the county in the process of doing this work. But the research and eagle-eye scrutiny is not aimed at prosecuting anyone but to make recommendations for better governance, and to reinvigorate civil society activity and action at the county. Similarly, more money for this project shall not be raised than is necessary to research, write the book, and disseminate the findings to the greater public in easy and real-time engagement through FrontlineSMS and other advanced technology tools. This will curb any temptation to bring down Tolgos Administration or to destroy the careers of good men and women working at the county.

Discussion

This article triggered an interest with me by the county bureaucrats and by the time I was compiling this work, I was in touch with several of them, especially in the Department of Tourism, where I strongly proposed cultural mapping of the county to serve as a guide for cultural planning and for promotion of tourism.

Switch from Grains (Maize) to Fruits (Avocado) Is Bankruptcy of Economic Ideas

Monday 03 December 2018

It did not come to me as a surprise that such backward thinking of changing from grains to fruits is prevalent among our policy-makers. The proposal is tantamount to economic suicide because there is no guarantee of a consistent market and also the movement of our people from subsistence farming to modern life where you play with finances to meet all your basic needs is a gradual process. We still have grain granaries that act as a savings account in case of economic difficulties.

Thus, the suggestion is like moving all the people from agricultural to industrial life all at once. And the people we are talking about are the most vulnerable in the society, devoid of any educational or skill support mechanisms. In addition, the means for this transitioning have not been indicated.

But we should acknowledge the fact that fruits are perishable. Grains are not perishable. And that the problem is not lack of market but lack of marketing. The problem again is not more of lack of marketing, but obstructed distribution. We farm for the Government. We do not farm for the market. So, improper distribution of the maize grain in Kenya from where it is plenty to where it is scarce is the first reason why this switch is problematic. After all, as a country we have not met the very basic requirements of food security.

The second reason is lack of mechanization and *technologization* of maize farming to free the farmers from daily hard work to looking for markets. This will go hand to hand with enhancing intensive agri-business education for the farmers and consolidation of farms by running them as companies limited by shares at both individual and community levels, and enhancing value-addition. This is where cooperatives are strongly recommended.

Finally, the most important shift should be from present approaches to farming to industrialization. The policy-makers should concentrate on industrializing Kenya so that farming will be left to those who are capable of doing it properly.

Discussion

There was a heated debate about the political implication of this conversation. The politicians who suggested this switch from maize to avocado defended themselves by saying that they rooted for general diversification in local agriculture, which was deemed a good policy proposal.

Little Emphasis on Qualified Employees by County Public Service Board (CPSB)

Monday 03 December 2018

I had an opportunity to study County Assembly committee report of 01 October 2015 on the activities of the County Public Service Board (CPSB) in 2014.

I found out that there is little emphasis on qualified employees. According to the report CPSB pays no attention at all to special skills that the county might require to develop. A lot of attention is paid on harmonizing employment numbers across the four sub-counties (Marakwet East, Marakwet west, Keiyo North, and Keiyo South), although the numbers do not proportionately add up.

The other observation is that there is poor on-the-job trainings for the staff to deliver on their tasks. The County Assembly committee report recommends that the budgetary allocation for staff trainings be utilized (in order to improve productivity of the staff together with implementation of sound performance contracts). However, I did not access follow-up and follow-on reports. They will form the subject of further enquiry through interviews and other research methodologies.

Finally, tomorrow Tuesday 04 December 2018 I will focus on EMC employments at the national government by studying Public Service Commission (PSC) ethnic balance in employment reports in order to ascertain the role of EMC leaderships in enhancing the participation of their people in the national government and inter-governmental organizations like the UN agencies.

Leader of Senate Majority Position is a Scam

Tuesday 04 December 2018

As promised yesterday that I was going to look at participation of EMC in national government and inter-governmental organizations such as the UN agencies, I was shocked that in the period 2013/2014, 2014/2015, 2015/2016, 2016/2017 of Public Service Commission (PSC) reports (www.publicservice.go.ke), participation of EMC is negligible, but worse among the Marakwet people.

I tried to dig deeper in the 2017/2018 period and found out that it is even worse than before, with the Marakwet not leading any constitutional office at all. Then I concluded that Marakwet people being placated with a non-constitutional office of the leader of the majority in the Senate which does not enable their people to advance in the national government and inter-governmental organizations is a successful hoax. The Marawet people should demand answers.

Next, still with EMC participation in the national government, I will explore EMC in commercial activities, especially award of major tenders/ contracts by critically examining IFMIS and other resources.

EMC Does Not Exercise Power at the National Government

Wednesday 05 December 2018

As promised yesterday that today I was going to scrutinize IFMIS and other resources to check participation of EMC in the national government commercial activities, I would like to report that I found out that no *EMCian* or company has been awarded a contract of value more than KES 100 million (USD 1 million) in the period 2013-2018.

Such contracts make it possible to create employment opportunities by building private sector entities that can employ competitively, and also enhance the bargaining power of EMC in the national government. Since this is the role of the leadership, I can state in no uncertain terms that *the leaders have slept on the job*.

Because such tender awards demonstrate heightened participation in the national government by our people, I can equally conclude that the economic foundations of EMC in this period are very weak, hence a lost decade, 2013-2022.

Mango Factory is the Worst Industrial Attempt

Thursday 06 December 2018

I managed to do some research on the proposed Tot Mango Factory (fruit factory). I can state categorically that apart from Sunny Mango Processors in Kambiti (Embu-Murang'a border) that does concentrates for Cocacola, there is no evidence of any other successful mango factory in Kenya. The much publicized Makueni County mango factory was not operational at the time of this reporting.

In 2012 I went to Cocacola asking them to establish a mango mini-processor in Kerio Valley. They replied me that I did not understand what I was asking. They referred me to Technoserv that does a lot of training for farmers and marketing of farm produce. Technoserv said that a processor in Kerio Valley could not be sustained on two major counts:
(i) irregular supplies, and
(ii) poor quality of mangoes.
Our mangoes are seasonal and that the processor will be rendered idle a greater part of the time, compromising with its viability. They suggested growing yellow passion in addition.

The quality of the mangoes in the Kerio Valley is not good. They suggested a variety like *ngowe*. All this time the market earmarked was Cocacola. I was not satisfied. Then they referred me to Sunny Mango Processors, which introduced the third element: (iii) marketing. If Cocacola refuses to buy the mango concentrates who else can buy them? How will you secure that alternative market? This is exactly what caused the redundancy of the Makueni County mango factory.

The options for Kerio Valley farmers are [1] solar drying of mangoes to make mango flakes, and [2] improving the mango varieties then sell them raw. But as a long-term plan the farmers can major in all-round maturing fruit varieties in order to sustain a fruit factory.

Therefore, the money put into a mango factory at Tot could have been utilized to put up more job-creating and industrial type industries like textiles and leather, the Kitui County case. Such industries have reliable supplies because they can even be imported and are capable of employing many people.

Discussion

This reporting was bitterly contested with the Managing Director of Kerio Valley Development Authority (KVDA) Mr David Kimosop who is in charge of the entire factory process questioning my commercial credentials. I posed a question, is there business or economic thinking outside common sense? No one responded to this question, nor did anyone give a counter argument. However, some evidence that for the factory to be operational there was need to have at least one million mango trees of the earmarked variety, and that KVDA and partners were going to import mangoes from other regions or countries to ensure that the factory is operational because even without some credible statistics, the number of mango trees in the Kerio Valley are hardly 100,000, even without discussing whether they are of the right and earmarked variety. It did not go down well in the observation that there is no region that had major variation in mango harvesting to Kerio Valley. I joined the discussion by observing that mango farming as a cash crop in the Kerio Valley was equally the most primitive policy-making. I observed that despite prevailing violent cattle rustling in the Kerio Valley, there were more goats per household than mango trees per household in the Kerio Valley.

EMC Propaganda Economy

Friday 07 December 2018

I would like to recast on propaganda economy.

There is a lot of fake news consumed by the residents of EMC. This news is propagated by some of the brightest who happen to be outside the county payroll. One of the most successful propaganda outlets that EMC residents are ready for paid subscription is EMC ASSEMBLY, a Whatsapp group.

I was told that there are in excess of 100 very promising group social media platforms. KAPCHEMUTWA administrative ward group is rated as the most progressive welfare congregation with an ability to raise millions of Kenya shillings towards economic development.

I propose formalization and commercialization of all viable of such groupings, with members subscribing at a fee, and then the groups are compelled to pay taxes to the county.

Discussion
Some members of the audience thought that this proposal of taxing social media groups was taken too far. They were against it. However, I gave the case of Uganda that introduced taxation of all social media platforms in the second half of 2018.

Agriculture Can Never Be the Backbone of Future EMC Economy, Tourism Should Be

Saturday 08 December 2018

I would like to make some observations on what should be the foremost economic concentration of EMC.

While Kenya touts agriculture as a lifeline of her economy, albeit without serious thought about its modernization, it is naive for EMC to follow after a similar fashion. The agricultural activities in EMC are at best rudimentary, and present and future land contestations shall never allow for modernized agriculture. In light of this I propose making tourism a core investment of the county on two major realizations:
(i) developing cost-effectively micro-tourist destinations in every village by sensitizing the residents rigorously to embrace a more hospitable and strategic system of values towards visitors, and
(ii) collapsing all the existing departments under tourism, or just introducing a tourist angle in all of them. The person in charge of tourism qualifies to be the deputy governor. In addition, there will be need to introduce such sub-departments as Forest Tourism and Sex Tourism

Changing the attitudes and perceptions of the local communities to look at development as an extension of hospitality has the indirect benefit of making the residents more entrepreneurial; thus enabling faster economic empowerment.

In my estimation, with proper mapping of the county, it is possible to have up to ten unique tourist attractions in every village, which shall encompass both tangible and intangible heritage.

All modern development is an extension of hospitality!

EMC Semi-Pastoral Economy. Is There Anything to Write Home?

Sunday 09 December 2018

I would like to focus on the semi-pastoral economy.

The residents of the Kerio Valley are semi-pastoral, keeping cattle and still practising cattle rustling, especially in Marakwet East. The violent cattle rustling activities, though negligible by human-loss measures, have served to taint the image of the county and scare off investors. Part of the reason is sensational media coverage that does not take into consideration overall county interest.

I propose that EMC invests in the pastoral economy under the Department of Agriculture by a serious thought of agricultural security through acquisition of such facilities and equipment as night vision drones with real-time feed to help in mobilization of security forces.

Cattle rustling is the third form of EMC cancer after nepotism and corruption.

EMC Still a County of Champions?

Monday 10 December 2018

I was both impressed and provoked by some social media posts about how we are both a county of champions and that of losers. Then I asked myself, are we truly still a county of champions?

In November 2012 at a seminar on sport and local development at St. Patrick's High School-Iten Bro. Colm O'Connell who founded the first athletics camp in Kenya at Iten in 1989 politely suggested that as a country we should embrace education instead of examinations. (His remarks "My Experiences as an Athletics Coach in Kenya" were published in Education Tomorrow - Kenya https://www.amazon.com/Education-Tomorrow-Kenya-Number-May-August-ebook/dp/B076L1S93Q/ref=mp_s_a_1_5?ie=UTF8&qid=154434 2190&sr=8-5&pi=AC_SX236_SY340_QL65&keywords=education+tomorrow +kenya&dpPl=1&dpID=51YmQqxpcAL&ref=plSrch and his athletics camp has produced some of the finest world record champions such as Vivian Cheruiyot in the 2008 Daegu Olympics.) From him, I learned that EMC produced the first married woman athlete Jepyator Thompson.

With limited budget and a high sense of purpose Bro. Colm O'Connell and his team consistently produced world record holders. Can we emulate the same with our present budget and develop EMC?

Discussion
I was made to understand that Jepyator Thompson has been procuring scholarships for students from EMC to study in the US.

Who Are EMC Anti-Colonial Heroes?

Tuesday 11 December 2018

I tried to wrestle with the question of EMC anti-colonial resistance. I was spurred by a conversation with a Pokot elder and by EMC Governor's 2018 *Mashujaa Day* (20 0ctober) speech.

The Pokot elder narrated to me that when his people refused to pay hut tax to the colonial administration they were punished by being asked (i) to fill an empty half a liter capacity cup with human tears, and (ii) to fill a similar empty container with a live colony of fleas. The Governor in his speech did not mention EMC anti-colonial resistance struggle.

The EMC people fought the colonials, as exemplified by
[1] the killing of 42 Nubians and a sergeant at Chebilil in Marakwet East in 1900,
[2] the killing of a colonial administrator by a Keiyo resistance fighter Arap Chemorin who sought refuge in Marakwet East, leading to the colonial administration burning down of huts in Kiptakitwa and Kabarsiran villages in 1914, and subsequent establishment of colonial administration headquarters at Chesewew in Marakwet East,
[3] the burning of huts at Sibow Village in Marakwet East by colonial police in 1914 because a Sibow man called Kimwalei threatened to destroy the colonial administration post at Ribo (Kolloa) in Tiaty Constituency, Baringo County,
[4] the Kolloa Affray/ massacre of 1950 that involved the people of Marakwet,
[5] the execution of Kimolei a Marakwet artist as quoted by Ngugi wa Thiong'o in his prison diary - the body of Kimolei has not been recovered, or
[6] the forcible acquisition of land from the Keiyo people in the Grogan Concession and the people's resistance against colonial settlers, with the complaints made to the Kenya Land Commission of 1932.

Should we care about anti-colonial freedom fighters?

Why Tolgos Will Get into Even More Trouble Soon

Wednesday 12 December 2018

I would like to look at Tolgos' recent detente with his critics.

Tolgos Administration soon will be marred by 2022 politics. However, the successful detente with his fierce critics in recent times will not guarantee the desired stability for economic development as Tolgos desires. He needs to follow his verbal remarks with tangible incorporation of his critics into his development agenda either directly or indirectly.

I suggest putting most of them into the board of county public corporations like (i) Rimoi Park, (ii) health facilities, (iii) schools, or (iv) county factories and other flagship economic entities. The smarter ones can be incorporated into an amorphous directorate of advisory to the Governor. This should equally be matched with other genuine reforms like meritocracy and guided tendering processes to maximize on the potential for heightened development.

Tolgos is not off the hook yet. But a consensus on the need to develop the county has been reached.

Discussion
While there were loud talk and complaints about poor leadership in EMC, I did not come across a more plausible proposal for curing that problem. There was no alternative leader suggested. There was no alternative development approach recommended. However, the proceedings of public participation and engagement were not disclosed or put in a way that can easily be judged.

Cattle Chips versus Human Chips: The Limits of Technological Ethics

Thursday 13 November 2018

I noted some follow-up comments on my earlier post on semi-pastoral economy. Some of the feedback entails using biometric chips inserted into livestock for identification and tracking using coordinate system. Earlier I had suggested application of infrared enabled drones for surveillance.

As a rejoinder I asked if it was possible to use human chips instead of animal chips because the animals are innocent after all. I know the application of Artificial Intelligence (AI) in curbing cattle rustling raises serious ethical and privacy challenges like biased data or biased training of the machines. But can we collect and input all fundamental data about the people of Kerio Valley, especially Pokot and Marakwet, into intelligent machines?

While cattle rustling is an economy that needs to be substituted with an alternative economy, can advanced technology curb cattle rustling or cause suffering to the semi-pastoralists?

Gorillas in Rimoi Park

Friday 14 December 2018

As an addition to the tourism economy, I would like to focus on introduction of both rare and endangered species in the Rimoi tourist destination.

As much as we want to diversify away from wild animals to other attractions, I suggest that we sample and buy some species such as gorillas in central Africa, panda in China, among others as part of the attraction delicacies in the park, but on a sustainable basis. We can also identify some special species that are indigenous to EMC like monkeys and turn them into diplomatic tools by rigorous domestication, marketing and exchanges.

Isn't EMC a virgin land?

Land Demarcation Will Make EMC Poorer

Saturday 15 December 2018

Today I focus on land adjudication, consolidation, and demarcation, which are the most contentious issues about EMC development.

I would like to begin by observing that if we label stages of human development simplistically as agrarian, industrial, technological, and information ages, and that we live in information era in 21st century, land is not very useful in enhancing our collective living conditions. In information period land is best left for public infrastructural development, preservation and beautification of the environment, and for agricultural and other major investments by those who like farming and/ or are capable of using land effectively.

By this realization:
(i) land demarcation will delay transition of our people into industrial, technological and *informatization* developments because it will put more emphasis on land than on information and knowledge;
(ii) demarcation will lead to fragmentation of land, making it commercially unviable. This will hasten poverty by giving rise to squatters out of people who shall sell their land to those who have money; and
(iii) land demarcation will create socio-political instability because of contests over boundaries and extent of clan lands in the process of consolidating small pieces.

Therefore, instead of demarcating land, let's move our people to commercial centers where we can provide them with modern facilities like good education, access to information and health care, among others, in the process of creating a large consumption market out of them.

EMC Witness to Transformation

Sunday 16 December 2018

This is an observation about EMC between 1911 and 1963. In May 2011 (100 years later) I stood before students of Tambach (Boma) High School and witnessed the endurance of the vision of our pioneer leaders in the colonial period who had made it a priority to build a Government African School at Tambach.

In 1911 EMC was subdued and put under colonial administration in the Kerio Province (Suk-Kamasia Reserve) ran from Eldama Ravine. In 1917-18 it was put under Uasin Gishu District in Nzoia Province administered from Naivasha. In 1924-25 the Elgeyo Local Native Council and Marakwet Local Native Council were formed, with their first sessions in September 1925. (See the list of councilors in my blog http://marakwetculture.blogspot.com/2011/11/marakwet-councillors-13-september-1925.html and in the annex). In 1931-32 the local native councils were amalgamated to form the Elgeyo Marakwet African District Council (ADC), where we had such prominent names as Kite arap Tiren, Chepterit arap Keture, and Chemweno arap Chebor. In May 1963 the ADC joined the expansive Sirikwa County that survived until after the recommendations of the Hardacre Commission of 1966.

Throughout the colonial administration our elected and nominated politicians upheld a superior focus towards socio-economic transformation of their people. Can we borrow something from them in the transformation of EMC?

The Future of Business is Small Business

Monday 17 December 2018

I focus on what, in my view, constitutes the future of business.

The availability of information and technology for common good makes it possible for everyone to run a business in a small and unique way over the Internet. At the moment big technology companies are only big because they have gone on a rampage of buying small companies because to make a big technology company constitutes different aspects of start-up technologies. The top seven global technology and e-commerce companies (Amazon, Google, Microsoft, Facebook, Baidu, Alibaba, and Tencent) work on assemblage of several different aspects of technological knowledge pursued by many diverse start-up technology companies or experts. In recent times all these technologies have applied Artificial Intelligence (AI).

In the case of EMC, instead of pursuing traditional big flagship projects, it is fair enough to work on enhancing development of professionally run small businesses by sourcing for technology and arranging for availability of reliable Internet connection in every village. The Internet of Things (IoT) [where a fridge can inform the owner at workplace that the food is running out] or 5G [with the fastest and massive connections] work best in the Internet plus economies of 21st century.

Discussion
In the conversations one of the audience observed that Kenya is still grappling with installation and application of 3G technologies, and a discussion of 5G technologies was misplaced.

Mega Developments as Community Investments

Tuesday 18 December 2018

I would like to follow up on a discussion about the Arror and Kimwarer hydropower projects which I was involved in one of the EMC forums.

I realized that there was a serious conflict between the communities and the proponents of the projects. I suggested that
   a. the communities be organized into groups/ limited liability companies and, according to the law, the value of their contributions like land and other resources be quantified then be made joint owners on that basis;
   b. the communities can invest in the projects through the county government; or
   c. the communities can seize the hydropower generation idea from the proponents then look for funding from financial institutions, a developer/ contractor and an operator of the hydropower generation installation, then sign a Power Purchase Agreement (PPA) from the Energy Regulatory Commission (ERC) under the fit-in-tariffs program – to generate and sell power through the utility Kenya Power.

In my view, the idea of "displacement by cash compensation in 21st century is not only a raw deal to communities, but is also primitive policy-making".

Put into consideration that generating hydropower is application of 19th century technology.

Rise of Female Politicians a Sign of EMC Transformation

Wednesday 19 December 2018

I look at the transformation of EMC female political power.

The first EMC woman politician was Miriam Chepto who was nominated to the Elgeyo Marakwet African District Council (ADC) in 1957 and was replaced by Naomi Kipyab in 1961. Although the number of female politicians across the political spectrum between 1963 and 2012 did not grow exponentially, the implementation of the New Constitution 2010 has given rise to many nominated female politicians from 2013.

However, in nominal terms, female versus male political power in EMC still raises some serious catch-up questions.

Still a Long Way to Universal Access to Safe, Clean (Drinking) Water in EMC

Thursday 20 December 2018

I make some observations on access to safe, clean (drinking) water.

In the quest for safe, clean (drinking) water the Katalel Dam in Keiyo North Sub-County was completed in 1927, combat against pollution of Kaptagat Forest water tower was initiated in 1954, and installation of water treatment plant was effected in 1955; Arid and Semi-Arid Lands (ASAL) water provision program under the District Focus for Rural Development (DFRD) as mooted in the 1980s helped in piping clean water to communities. In addition, there was the inclusion of water component in the Constituency Development Fund (CDF) in the mid-2000s, among other initiatives that put the Ministry of Water at the core.

The efforts of the county government in the provision of safe, clean (drinking) water is far from satisfactory, as exemplified by the recent water scarcity protests at Kapsowar Shopping Centre. However, while access to safe, clean (drinking) water is included in the Sustainable Development Goals (SDGs) as Goal 6 (clean water and sanitation), I will not dwell on what one of the pundits opined that with respect to EMC we should be discussing how far we have come along in implementing Millennium Development Goals (MGDs), not transitioning into SDGs.

Policy Miracles Needed to Make Some Progress on the EMC Integrated Development Plan (CIDP), 2018-2022

Friday 21 December 2018

I will begin today to look at the County Integrated Development Plan, 2018-2022.

After going through the 388 pages that make the plan and relating with the stated theme, I should let you know that it is a *welfare plan*, *not* an *industrialization plan*.

While the idea and spirit of the CIDP is good, in my view, it needs some magic to get it realized. Out of the about KES 144 billion needed to implement it, KES 15 billion are internal sources, while the rest KES 128 billion come from external sources, mostly from national government and development partners (donors).

In my view, the only most viable external sources of capital for industrialization are Foreign Direct Investments (FDIs) that come with both money, management expertise, and advanced technology to create employment opportunities for the youth, hence enhancing county purchasing power. Because the idea of the CIDP is not geared towards industrialization of the county, but social welfare, attracting FDIs will be a tall order. Thus, realizing the CIDP in the form it is needs some miracle.

Discussion

This reporting raised some concerns with the county government bureaucrats with some of them indicating that many experts, especially from World Bank and United Nations, had reviewed and praised the plan; however, they were at a loss when asked to name the experts.

EMC Government Should Apologize for Misleading Sections of CIDP, 2018-2022

Saturday 22 December 2018

I focus on the County Integrated Development Plan (CIDP), 2018-2022, energy (infrastructure) component.

While there is an ambitious plan to power at least 80% of EMC (households) from the current 30% estimate, there are no clear-cut measures advanced towards meeting that target at the county level. Depending entirely on the national government to meet that target makes the CIDP with respect to that component at best whimsical. However, as the plan envisages development and promotion of clean forms of energy (p. 79, section 4.4.1.6), I propose a focus on small scale solar PV at residential and commercial premises.

Since the publishing of CIDP is 2018, the section that indicates that Arror and Kimwarer hydropower dams are under construction is misleading, and even if they are under construction, there is no explanation as to whether the power generated from them would be used *expressly* to meet the CIDP's 80% estimate access to electricity (by households) by 2022:

"… there are two hydroelectric dams *under construction* by Kerio Valley Development Authority (KVDA) at Arror and Kimwarer, which are projected to generate 45 and 20 Megawatts respectively *to the national grid*" (p. 12).

This demands an apology from the county government!

There is also over-concentration on electricity at the expense of cheaper forms of energy that can meet the county's needs towards industrialization. Electricity is an energy carrier, not a form of energy, thus it is bound to be expensive.

Discussion

This reporting was taken seriously by the county government when it was indicated in subsequent conversations that there was a higher likelihood that the county government will be sued for publishing an erroneous plan. And by the time of compiling these reports, the CIDP, 2018-2022, had been pulled down from Elgeyo Marakwet County Government website.

Pre-School and Vocational Education Can Transform EMC

Sunday 23 December 2018

Still with the County Integrated Development Plan (CIDP), 2018-2022, today I look at Early Childhood Development and Education (ECDE) and Technical and Vocational Education Training (TVET).

The work of the county government in these areas is commendable (pp. 22-23, 94, 152, 225). The physical infrastructure and enrolment has moved from nearly nothing to something in the period 2013-2017, and there are plans underway to scale it up further by an injection of about KES 500 million (p. 145) in the period 2018-2022. This has the double effect of improving literacy and employability of the youth.

However, there is need to synchronize the work of the county government in these realms with other related plans such as training and capacity building, and civic education and citizen participation that have limited budgetary allocation (pp. 137, 150). This will help in covering the much cited too much concentration on physical infrastructure instead of capacity building (p. 59) and lack of innovative proposals on Income Generating Activities (IGAs) (p. 60) listed as some of the challenges in the implementation of the CIDP, 2013-2017.

In the case of vocational education, there is need to *technologize* the programs as an improvement to the conduct of the traditional courses in order to suit the needs of modern industry and to enable the students to find relevance in many job market listings.

There is Limited Commercialization of Forest Resources in the EMC CIDP, 2018-2022

Monday 24 December 2018

I would like to look at forest resources and its linkage with environment and climate change, and water and sanitation from a commercial angle.

The forest cover in EMC is among the largest (on per capita landmass) in the country at 30.93%. The total cover is 936.91 square kilometers [93691.28 hectares; 1 hectare = 0.01 square kilometers] (p. 16) against the total land area in the county at 3029.6 square kilometers (p. 4).

There is planned investment in the conservation of the forest resources for provision of water, and prevention against adverse effects of climate change. The total planned financial resources to be expended in the CIDP, 2018-2022, are about KES 330 million (p. 103). However, there is no plan advanced towards recovering that money, either by sale of water, sale of wood and medicinal resources, or forest tourism, etc.

As much as conservation of the forest is for public good and is intended to support many other economic activities such as agriculture, *conservation without commercialization is a waste of public resources.*

Energy and Mineral Resources Should Not Be a Major Concentration of EMC

Tuesday 25 December 2018

I would like to focus on oil and gas, and minerals in the County Integrated Development Plan (CIDP), 2018-2022. The energy and mineral resources discussed in the CIDP, 2018-2022, are oil and gas, fluorite, marble/ limestone, gold, sand, construction stones (p. 14).

Although there are no comprehensive geological maps utilizing modern technologies about EMC, a focus on oil resources is a misplaced priority. First, unless Kenya/ Africa embarks on industrialization, the transition of the global economies into Fourth Industrial Revolution (Industrialization 4.0) that puts emphasis on cheaper ways of generating electricity (especially from coal and natural gas) or a sustained quest for clean and efficient forms of electricity (nuclear, solar, wind, hydro, hydrogen, waves) will compromise with demand for oil. However, the available oil and gas resources will be used in the refineries to make chemicals. Second, oil and gas in Kerio Valley will most likely lead to resource curse (conflict) over scramble for land. Third, the EMC ecology is fragile for oil and gas production or other scaled up mining activities like gold.

Discussion

There was enhanced exploration of oil and gas resources in the Kerio Valley by Tullow Inc. It was difficult to convince the discussants that such activities were meant just for political expediency by the Government and for adding to the petroleum reserves of such oil exploration and production companies to enhance the competitiveness of their shares in financial markets. The Government of Kenya used transported crude oil, which the Government made deliberate losses owing to the low per barrel oil prices at the time, in my view, to attract investments and interest in the marginalized northern regions, especially Turkana County.

Agriculture Component of County Integrated Development Plan (CIDP), 2018-2022

Wednesday 26 December 2018

I would like to focus on the agriculture component of the CIDP, 2018-2022, by observing that despite the challenges of fragile ecology, insecurity, small pieces of land, lack of talent, among others (pp. 12-14), implementing the agricultural component of the CIDP will reach moderate modernization of agriculture in the county.

The plan targets improved productivity, good earnings, and food security (p. 118), and intends to invest in them by focusing on a wide variety of activities chief among which are irrigation farming, soil conservation, and combat against crop and animal pests and diseases. These are comprehensively spelled out (pp. 118-120, 121-126, 311-336).

However, modernizing agriculture should not necessarily be about value addition, use of Artificial Insemination (AI) and improved breeds, or mechanization (p. 64, 69), it should entail a wholesome rethink of the ideological and philosophical conduct of agriculture in the county; for example, organizing farmers to invest as a group (other than through cooperatives, p. 24), sourcing for land and market away from the county to cultivate and meet food security and other strategic requirements.

EMC CIDP, 2018-2022, Is an Additional Challenge on the Challenges of CIDP, 2013-2017

Thursday 27 December 2018

I evaluate the CIDP, 2018-2022, by observing that it does not strive to address the challenges of CIDP, 2013-2017, as spelled out in chapter three (pp. 44-61) of the report, but serves as a cumulative of the mistakes of the CIDP, 2013-2017, necessitating a complete overhaul of the plan.

First, the CIDP, 2018-2022, should strive to beat the averages of national and global development indicators. EMC falls short of most averages of prevailing national and global development measures such as poverty, literacy, doctor to patient ratio, teacher to student ratio, among others.

Second, the CIDP, 2018-2022, is not based on concrete development indicators backed up by credible statistics. There is no accurate per capita water usage, energy usage, health care utilization, technology uptake, gross/per capita impact of cattle rustling/ insecurity, among others.

Finally, the CIDP, 2018-2022, should aim at curing (financial) resource deviations in the CIDP, 2013-2017 (KES 44 billion against actual KES 17 billion) instead of introducing other crazy (financial) resource gaps (KES 144 billion against a projected actual KES 15 billion).

All these challenges can be ameliorated in two major ways: (1) converting the CIDP, 2018-2022, from a plan to a policy guideline, or (2) redesigning the CIDP, 2018-2022, from the current welfare outlook into an EMC industrialization plan by critically examining the drawbacks of the CIDP, 2013-2017, and citizen dissatisfaction about service delivery.

Suspicion about Ghost Workers in EMC Can Be Cured by Technological Verification

Friday 28 December 2018

I try to reflect on the suspicion of the presence of ghost workers by proposing adoption of modern technology in order to eliminate any ghost workers, deter future inclusion of ghost workers in the payroll, and ascertain the implications of such happenings.

First, I would like to observe that presence of ghost workers, if any, is a reflection of mismanagement of county affairs because the total workforce in the county is hardly 2,000 and that the county is grappling with how to reduce them to increase money channeled to actual development.

Second, presence of ghost workers, if any, is because of lack of clearly delineated occupational descriptions. What does the county want? Whom do they want? When do they want?

Finally, presence of ghost workers, if any, is a criminal complicity. All ghost workers should be related to certain bureaucrats by blood or by certain interests.

To eradicate ghost workers and to ameliorate public perception about suspected ghost workers, there is need to adopt some human resources and payroll technologies that, without jeopardizing the privacy of the workers, can instill confidence in the county management system.

Alleviating Every Challenge in EMC by Industrialization and Urbanization

Saturday 29 December 2018

I revisit some of the issues raised in my previous reporting.

First, there was discussion about cattle rustling activities in Marakwet East; second, there was encroachment of riparian lands and water conservation towers in upland areas as a result of limited arable land due to population explosion and further land fragmentation; and, third, there was a wider challenge of maize prices and economic viability of maize farming and the need for crop diversification to alternatives such as the weird fruit (avocado) suggestion.

In one of the responses I proposed curing most of such serious challenges by embarking on industrialization and urbanization – we recreate urban centers, build industrial systems there and enforce forced migration of people. The idea of urbanization should be planned meticulously to avoid (i) ghost towns, and (ii) socio-psychological challenges as a result of drastic lifestyle and other changes.

Urbanization will create good consumers out of the people, whereas industrialization will create good workers out of them.

Discussion

The members of the audience were strongly against forced migration of people. They recommended public participation and democratic persuasion, which I thought was tantamount to applying delay tactics in matters of great importance. I argued that the reason people elect to have leaders is because they fear to make decisions. So, the leaders should at all times be able to think and make decisions for their subjects.

Is Artificial Intelligence (AI) a Threat?

Sunday 30 December 2018

In the course of this month I was hard pressed to explain my fancy with Artificial Intelligence (AI).

A member of the book project audience began by saying that I loved machines more than human beings. Another one said that I was anti-Christ by inferring to use of chips inserted on human beings.

I must observe that Artificial Intelligence (AI) is a new frontier of technological revolution in the scale of electricity about 100 years before. Its real application, especially utilization of neural networks in Natural Language Processing (NLP) and machine translations, began late 2016. I, like most other AI enthusiasts and practitioners, believe that AI will complement our overcoming human struggles and, in most part, will free human beings from physical and mental drudgery.

However, without diligence in the work of data scientists, AI engineers, and other practitioners, it might come with very serious ethical challenges such as (1) biased data and biased training of machines, (2) massive unemployment/ lay-offs, (3) wider income and wealth inequality between individuals and nations, with China and USA being at the top because of access to massive data for training the machines, or (4) rise of autonomous weapons, spelling doom to humankind.

§Although I keep studying business (supply chain management) and computer science (Artificial Intelligence), I recognize the impending loss of traditional professions and occupations. It is no longer enough to be conversant in one area of specialization because a wide range of these professions are fast being replaced by AI. At the end of 2011 together with the late B E Kipkorir (a foremost EMC intellectual) I recognized the necessity of a shift from a single specialization to multi-disciplinary engagements, hence the beginning of multi-disciplinary conferences at Kipchumba Foundation. For instance, a manager who is not conversant with AI has no future in management. Similarly, I have witnessed many young people performing tasks that they were not trained originally.

Fear of technology is a swipe card to poverty and backwardness.

Discussion

This discussion appeared a new introduction to the members of the audience, with some of them indicating that AI will never come to Africa, or that it's upon future generations to grapple with it. Others observed that AI might widen socio-economic inequality between individuals. With respect to the latter I argued that the data should be monopolized by the governments and AI should be treated as a public good.

Tearing Apart Prevailing Amorphous Sense of Status Quo in EMC Will Create Room for the Rise of the Rest

Monday 31 December 2018

I would like to focus on abstract notions about county development that I experienced in the course of my interactions this month and think that they are priority issues to be guarded against in 2019.

First, a young man asked me to allow him to exit the book project Whatsapp group because his benefactor did not like me. Second, one of my friends and his followers became disagreeable to me because they thought that I stole their ideas and formed a parallel Whatsapp group to both undermine their work and to antagonize them.

In the first case, I allowed the young man to exit the group and asked him to reappear in another mobile telephone number by following the group link. In the process, I posed a question to my good friend Ronald Chogii who is an academic at the University of Nairobi, School of Business, about that case. He denied that it does reflect on who we are (our values), but are just aspirations of certain insecure elite who had become too comfortable and overconfident in subverting the rise of young people by preventing them from exploring themselves and in accessing alternative ideas to support their youthful aspirations.

In the second case, I tried to put up a spirited defense that my entry into EMC discourse six years later served to complement the work of everyone because in all cases I only aim at offering voluntary public service and that my taking a black and white perspective does not help me in anyway. Most of my detractors were not convinced. Even if they are just a few individuals who can be contained, they appeared to me to be exceedingly brilliant and energetic people who should be redirected to contribute meaningfully to the development of the county.

To cure the illusion of status quo in a developing country and county such as ours, I propose an enablement of the rise of the rest to create as many centers of power and as many plutocrats as possible to champion certain issues and causes without petty politics standing in their way.

EMC Blame Game in Resolving Cattle Rustling

Tuesday 01 January 2019

I look at cattle rustling as a threat to the economic stability of the EMC and also as a compromising factor in the improvement of Human Development Index (HDI) about the county.

Some of the reasons advanced for not containing cattle rustling by the county government bureaucrats is that the security function is charged with the national government through the Ministry of Interior with the National Police Service (NPS) and the coordinators of national government as the foremost duty bearers. However, I am of the view that if we take that route, we shall not make any progress in resolving cattle rustling.

Cattle rustling is an economy, let's take the economic route.

EMC government can end cattle rustling singlehandedly by agreeing with the county governments of Baringo and West Pokot to initiate joint economic activities at the border. That is exactly what is happening between the Pokot and the Turkana through the efforts of the county governments of West Pokot and Turkana.

EMC should take Red Cross joint irrigation schemes as a playbook.

Anti-FGM Struggles Are of No Direct Economic Benefit to EMC

(Bonus Reporting: Tuesday 01 January 2019)

I patiently followed discussions against female circumcision in the book project Whatsapp group. Then I concluded that such debates, while good, cannot advance EMC as an economic power.

First, none of the discussants against FGM, including me, gave convincing evidence of relationships between poverty and FGM, poor school performance of the girl child and FGM, HIV/AIDS and FGM, early marriage/ school dropout and FGM, or difficulty in delivery and FGM; whereas those supporting FGM did not give evidential relationship between promiscuity and FGM.

Second, while I recognize the efforts of the pioneers of anti-FGM struggles, I am afraid that national and local policy-making and struggles against female circumcision is a waste of time and public resources.

Let's wait FGM out to end on its own.

Resolving Low Productivity in EMC

Wednesday 02 January 2019

I would like to highlight on the low productivity of EMC government workforce, as one its most serious bottlenecks towards economic transformation.

Most discussants in the book project Whatsapp group questioned *not* the *competence*, but the *productivity* of EMC government workforce. I suggest that the county government comes up with more concrete measures of measuring productivity of staff such as
- ✓ %contribution to county GDP,
- ✓ contribution to employment creation,
- ✓ number of visitors caused to EMC,
- ✓ amount of donor funds or joint programs secured,
- ✓ innovations/ patents registered, or
- ✓ number of start-ups and their success rates, among others.

All these should be supported by credible, real-time economic statistics and statistical projections. And those who produce should be rewarded, whereas those who fail to produce should be replaced with those who are more productive, while being encouraged to work hard through relevant trainings, counseling and other incentives.

The legacy of Governor Tolgos rests on resolving productivity issues.

EMC Needs Credible Economic Statistics

(Bonus Reporting: Wednesday 02 January 2019)

Questions have been raised about the statistics that inform policy thinking and planning in EMC.

While the availability or unavailability of accurate and reliable economic statistics cannot be verified at this stage, there is need also to move ahead and initiate real-time consumer price movements such as the prices of potatoes.

The county government should put more emphasis on research for planning purposes.

Without credible economic statistics, economic planning in EMC is a dangerous guesswork!

Regulation, Modernization, and Promotion of *Chang'aa* and *Busaa* Is the Way to Go for EMC

Thursday 03 January 2019

I was engaged in a moral debate about the place of indigenous alcohol economy. Two choices were presented: to suppress and abandon it, and to regulate and modernize it. I chose the latter.

I observed that even without the back-up of credible economic statistics at the county, which we lack anyway,
- ✓ *chang'aa* and *busaa* is the largest most liquid economy in EMC, and
- ✓ *chang'aa* and *busaa* is the second largest EMC industry after agriculture.

The regulation and modernization process should aim at
- ensuring hygiene and stable alcoholic content, and
- producing modern brands out of them and expanding market reach.

A bill that circumvents the narrow-mindedness of the Kiambu and Murang'a counties' inspired 2014 national alcohol bill should be introduced and passed through the EMC County Assembly by lumping all indigenous alcohol (*chang'aa, busaa,* honey mead/ *muratina,* food remains alcohol, among others) under *indigenous economy*:
1. many children have been and continue to be educated through *chang'aa* and *busaa,*
2. no social function has been successful without some form of alcohol,
3. rigorous regulation will curb irresponsible drinking, and
4. rehabilitation of alcoholics is irresponsible policy-making because it adds nothing directly to the coffers of EMC.

Discussion
I made this proposal as a way of recognizing all fundamental indigenous industries that show potential for modernization and scaling up. Among others, they include weaponry, household goods, medicine and surgery, water furrow, musical technologies. The proposal faced fierce resistance from the discussants who were of the view that all forms of alcohol should be banned in the county and all alcoholics should be rehabilitated. However, there was no economic proposal substitute advanced as a counter to modernization of the indigenous industries. There was only blanket condemnation. And I am strongly against blanket dismissal of policies without giving plausible alternatives.

Let's Develop Our Cooperatives

(Bonus Reporting: Thursday 03 January 2019)

I reviewed some responses on cooperative societies.

There was unanimity that forming, managing, and transforming cooperative societies in every industry will help EMC to move faster.

The cooperatives will help farmers and business people to learn and to accumulate capital.

I strongly urge the county government to focus on this area.

Managing cooperatives is one of the economic panaceas of *EMC!*

Discussion
This reporting garnered a lot of support with the members of the audience proposing that cooperatives be extended beyond agriculture to covering all aspects of consumer life, especially in commercial activities with controlled/ controllable market.

EMC Formalities versus Development

Friday 04 January 2019

I would like to look at the narrow-mindedness of development in EMC.

In two separate responses on the book Whatsapp group, two discussants responded to me regarding formalities. The first one said that the cattle rustling prone administrative wards do not have the money to invest in ending cattle rustling because the stipulations of a 2015 equalization of funds law (EDA) does not reflect such spending. The other discussant asked why youth and women support funds should be budgeted every year if the whole idea is to disburse funds without a follow-up concern if the projects for which money is being sought are implemented or not.

Both cases hinge on low staff productivity and lack of creativity among the leaders. Unless we move away from narrow understanding of the law, I doubt if we can make progress, if at all. There is no nation that has progressed on the basis of the law, nations move forward on the basis of consensus. The law is only a safeguard.

Economic development should be conducted according to local conditions, not dictates of the law.

Get Out, Get Down to Work

(Supplementary Reporting: Friday 04 January 2019)

I would like to take this opportunity to give a weekend piece of advice to the young people:
1-Let's get out of our comfort zones and seriously do the things that we are afraid to do
2-Let's work like donkeys and never waste time - given an opportunity, complement yourself with intelligent machines
3-Let's not waste our monies on luxuries – you will never change yourself or the world or make a name by being soaked in factory manufactures
4-Let's delay a little bit getting married to get quality education or a good job, or to build a business or a philanthropic set-up
5-Let's get a few and manageable number of children
6-Let's observe things keenly and resolve them steadfastly without emotions; let's not be afraid of boring details – they are what make for the difference
7-Let's focus on something that we like and work on it consistently over a long period of time
8-Let's not follow politicians, they waste our time; but if you decide to be a politician, aim at altering history
9-Let's have a consistent study, especially on the things that matter to us, but do complete reading of books or other materials, especially from good writers, and be wary of fake news or fancy quotations out of context
10-Let's focus on computer science as a second and major career path because the world in the coming years will be dominated by computer scientists or economies of computer programmers

Human life is lived only once and for a short time, let's use it to make history.

Establishing a "No Weapons Corridor" at Border Areas

(The second bill after "modernization of *chang'aa* and *busaa*")

Saturday 05 January 2019

I would like to summarize the discussions on violent cattle rustling activities by observing that there is need to introduce a 10-km wide security corridor with no any form of weapons allowed at the borders of Baringo, Elgeyo Marakwet and West Pokot counties.

I should be happy to draw a bill and pass through the county assemblies of Baringo, Elgeyo Marakwet and West Pokot. The bill aims at rigorous surveillance and security enforcement at the border areas by
-CCTV cameras using solar and remote control technology,
-Armed drones with infrared imaging,
-Facial detection and recognition of the residents,
-Military barbed wire fencing along the most critical sections of the corridor,
-Establishing paid and well equipped National Police Reservists, with night vision goggles, and
-Vetting all police and security persons deployed at the border areas.

Security is a local investment, it is not the responsibility of the national government.

Let's Move Our People to Commercial Centres Where We Can Provide Them with Modern Services

(The third proposed bill after "modernization of *chang'aa* and *busaa*", and "no weapons corridor")

(Bonus Reporting: Saturday 05 January 2019)

I would like to propose a bill that will move our people to the nearest commercial centers and compel the national and county governments to provide per household with modern facilities:
- a. Low cost houses
- b. Electricity
- c. Television set
- d. Tap water
- e. Internet
- f. Desktop computer/ laptop
- g. Washing machine and drier

Those who will continue farming will be free to cultivate their farms but are not allowed to live there or to use hand hoe.

A Mini Library in Every Ward in EMC

(The fourth proposed bill, after "modernization of *chang'aa* and *busaa*" and "no weapons corridor", and "urbanizing residents")

Sunday 06 January 2019

I suggest that let's build a mini library in every ward.

These mini libraries should help in promoting reading culture and in offering other fundamental services such as printing, preparation for examinations by students, applying for jobs or a place to waste time meaningfully by jobseekers.

We need mini libraries to prevent our people from relying on fake news.

Discussion

A whole discussion on establishing museums that can combine well with these suggested libraries was conducted. I supported it in the sense that it was like killing two birds with one stone.

Poverty Eradication Should Be the Rallying Agenda in EMC

Monday 07 January 2019

I would like to revisit some of the conceptual things that I believe fail in EMC.

What qualifies EMC government as a government?

From my interactions with the residents of EMC, everyone is just doing their own things. There is no unifying agenda pursued in EMC.

I should propose *poverty eradication* and ask that all medals and favors dished out should be on the basis of contribution to poverty eradication.

Discussion
I was asked what I mean by "everyone is just doing their own things". I replied that from my observation and interviews with the local people, civilian and county government efforts towards development of the county were not synchronized.

Let's Sue the Government in 2019 over Compensation for Cattle Rustling Losses

Tuesday 08 January 2019

I would like to revisit compensation of the victims of cattle rustling activities in EMC, especially in the Kerio Valley.

Slightly over two years ago (in 2016) Moses Kirop Chelang'a (a smart young lawyer from Kerio Valley) began drafting my affidavit as a victim of violent cattle rustling activities in the Kerio Valley. This year I reminded him about it and he has promised to revisit it.

Moses Chelang'a should be supported to sue the government in 2019.

Justice delayed is justice denied!

Discussion

In the discussion on one of the Kerio Valley social media groups, there was a suggestion that the government should be sued after cattle rustling stops. I observed that since cattle rustling is an economy, it will not stop but will transform.

Cable Cars without a Vibrant Tourism Economy Is Wrong

Wednesday 09 January 2019

I should like to recast at some of the economic fancies flaunted in EMC: a cable car.

At the moment there is poor purchasing power at the county, poorly developed tourism economy, unreliable power supply system, or rampant corruption that can compromise with smooth running of the cable cars.

Without good thinking, cable cars, or electric roller coasters are dangerous economic games.

Cable cars should succeed a vibrant tourism economy.

Discussion
An intense discussion over this observation ensued. The discussants were of the view that a cable car can be a standalone tourist attraction or that it can pull tourists to EMC. I classified cable cars under mobility tourism and some of the participants supported me by indicating that the transitioning of EMC into electrified mobility should be gradual and organized.

Developing a Tourist Attraction or an Equivalent Industrial System in Every Ward

(The fifth proposed bill after "modernization of *chang'aa* and *busaa*", "no weapons corridor", "urbanizing residents", and "a mini library in every ward")

Thursday 10 January 2019

I would like to follow up on my earlier writing that we should make tourism the backbone of EMC economy by preparing to draw a bill requiring the county government to develop at least one tourist attraction or an equivalent industrial system in every ward.

Let's have one tourist attraction or an equivalent industrial system in every ward.

Overconcentration on EMC Government Is Small Thinking

Friday 11 January 2019

I would like to consider the economic height of joining the county government. [I do not mean the county, but the government.]

If we assume that the harmonized average annual disbursement to EMC in the period 2013-2022 reaches KES 4 billion (USD 40 million), then the nominal financial total in that period is KES 40 billion (USD 400 million). We can assume further that that is the nominal annual revenue of a for-profit firm called EMC, thus EMC will not rank anywhere in global commerce. [But I do not underestimate the value of well invested KES 4 billion (USD 40 million) every year for 10 consecutive years. However, that is not the case with EMC six years later.]

From this observation, I should encourage young people to think big, invest hard and then donate to EMC, not banking on EMC government. That way, as a county and people, we can scale our ambitions further. It will also help us to avoid the present pettiness expressed in propaganda and showbiz/ Public Relations (PR) by a section of our elite.

Discussion
It was observed that there were no economic activities initiated by the county government in the period 2013-2018 that generated sufficient revenue to cover their initial costs over time. In simple terms, there were no county government investments that were verifiably functional.

The Idea of Building Museums in EMC Is Welcome but with Caution

(Supplementary Reporting: Friday 11 January 2019)

I would like to add my voice to the EMC attempts at building two museums. Why not build 20 small museums?

The Kenya's idea of building white elephant museums that bring no returns should be avoided in EMC. Let's build optimized economic systems:
1. Configure the museums to reflect specialized issues e.g. indigenous technology museum, pre-colonial art gallery, second world war museum, rare species museum, among others, or
2. Rigorously researched, innovated museum business systems.

Building a museum as a national duty should be resisted, we want museums as viable economic systems.

Discussion
An appropriate definition of a museum that accord with local conditions was non-existent. It serves it right to first conceptualize a local definition of a museum that absorbs the aspirations of the local residents. That will make the museum a sustainable outfit.

Missing Details of Modern Industry in EMC

Saturday 12 January 2019

I would like to look at the available details for transitioning to modern business as available in EMC.

Last weekend I had some interviews at Iten with some young people about their understanding of modern business. I realized that the young people were poorly versed on registration of companies; filing tax returns; import and export trade; applying for trademarks, patents and copyrights; improved sealing and packaging of goods.

The county government should lead in sensitizing the young people about modern business.

Myths of Youth Unemployment in EMC

Sunday 13 January 2019

I would like to look at two major discussions on youth unemployment and how to resolve it as discussed in the book project Whatsapp group.

First, I followed one thread that was of the view that youth unemployment can be resolved by imparting skills on the youth. The other involved asking youth to venture into self-employment by forming and running their businesses.

I was stupefied by both observations by noting that even with skills or money, the youth cannot create competitive employment opportunities for themselves, unless assisted by the county government. Equally, unless with the conscious and mercantilist efforts of the county government, it will be difficult to attract Foreign Direct Investments (FDIs) in EMC in order to create employment opportunities for the youth. The necessary infrastructure and incentives are needed for the latter.

There is nowhere on earth where a young person has created a job for themselves by themselves.

Discussion

It was observed that youth followed after about four categories: those educated and formally employed; those skilled and informally employed; those educated and skilled but jobless; and those with no education, skill or job. The latter is the most suffering lot. Energetic and health youth doing informal jobs such as lifting loads were classified under the skilled and informally employed category. In my view, to resolve the issue of youth unemployment, there is need for mobilization of people to work, even as cheap laborers.

Time for an Industrial EDA

Monday 14 January 2019

I would like to bring my thoughts to bear on the first county assembly bill on equalization of funds between wards, famously called Equitable Development Act (EDA), 2015.

In my view, it is time that the content of EDA be revised to give it an *industrial outlook* from the current welfare outlook. This revision should target modernization of indigenous industries, industrial systems in every ward, urbanization and transition into modern life, security as a local investment, among other fundamental service provision components.

The new EDA should aim at raising local standards and make EMC the centre of Kenya and a lesson for the world.

Shedding Tears for a Lost Proposed Kerio University

Tuesday 15 January 2019

I would like to reflect on the lost proposed Kerio University.

As I look back I see a trend of lost major projects due to petty political differences like the Kibaki Administration proposed referral hospital in Marakwet District. The Kerio University is no different. I nearly cried when proposed Kapenguria University graduated 250 Pokot children in 2018. EMC should have been in that league!

We need to educate our political leaders to look at things from a strategic perspective, not seeking for votes all the time, because, after all, they will lose an election at one point in time.

Discussion

I was asked how the proposed Kerio University was lost and who was responsible. I responded that, to the best of my knowledge, the Governor and Senator successfully ensured that it was lost because they initiated a tug of war between themselves on where it was supposed to be located, with a focus on their individual political re-election in 2017 general election. The grandstanding served to waste time until the government policy on expansion of universities was reversed.

Annex: Elgeyo Marakwet Councillors, 1925-1963

Introduction

[The listing between 1925 and 1932 covers members of the Marakwet Local Native Council (LNC), mostly.]

There have been twelve major new appointments to the Marakwet Local Native Council and Elgeyo-Marakwet African District Council (ADC) between 1925 and 1963. The appointments were made in 1925, 1928, 1931, 1935 (after amalgamation), 1941, 1945, 1948, 1950, 1954, 1957, and 1960. The appointments of 1925 were made through the powers of the Local Authority Ordinance of 1924. On 2 December 1944 the DC Tambach realized that the council had overrun its three-year term.

The elections were conducted in baraza by acclamation. Chiefs were only nominated and not elected. A woman was appointed to the council for the first time in 1957.

There are some spelling inconsistencies with some names like Ayabei/ Aiyabei, Kitei/ Kite, Mirriam/ Miriam. In addition, Gazette notice no. 1086 of 20 February 1962 appointed Chief Willie Kipto arap Chirchir to replace DC Elgeyo-Marakwet as the chairman to the council.

The existing locations were adjusted in 1957. The change was effected via DC's notice of 22 February 1957 as follows:
Mokoro and Endo were merged to form Endo
Sambirir remained unchanged
Talai and Kibuswa were merged into Moiben
Sengwer and Cherangany became Cherangany
Kapchemutwa, Irong and Mutei were merged into Irong
Valley areas of Rokocho, Marichor, Tumeyo and Metkei became Soy
Upper areas of Rokocho, Marichor, Tumeyo and Metkei formed Mosop.

Elgeyo-Marakwet African District Council joined Sirikwa County Council together with Nandi, Uasin Gishu, Trans Nzoia, and West Pokot on 1 May 1963 according to the 11 April 1963 letter circulated by the secretary to the council following the proceedings of the amalgamation meeting of Friday 24 November 1961.

The Councillors and their Developments

1. Government legal notice no. 393 of 23 September 1925

Twelve appointments were made to the council [the names were not visible from the reports]

2. Government legal notice no. 467 of 13 September 1928.

Elected:
Kipseswa arap Kitur
Kipsobuch arap Kaino
Kaburuet arap Kapchebos
Cherop arap Chesum
Chelanga arap Kipsanga
Yego arap Chepkorat

Nominated:
Yano arap Kipkech
Muruong'ot arap Sitienei
Chesseweo arap Kipteres
Kipkech arap Chelagat
Kisang arap Talai
Lokityang arap Lasero

Kipsobuch arap Kaino resigned and was replaced by Kirop arap Kipkeyo through government notice no. 142 of 27 February 1929. Kisang arap Talai replaced Cheboi arap Yego through government notice no. 510 of 25 July 1929. Yano arap Kipkech and Kaburuet arap Kapchebos resigned and were replaced by Kimengich arap Chelal and Kipchepkis arap Tegeroi by the government notice no. 736 of 9 December 1930.

3. Government legal notice no. September 1931

[The actual names could not be found]

4. Government legal notice no. 212 of 19 March 1935

Sixteen appointments:
Chepkok arap Kisang
Chesire arap Kipkuto
Chebi arap Bomonei
Chelanga arap Kiborus
Kipkoisin arap Kanda
Kipkese arap Ruto
Sero arap Cheso
Kiyai Kimagarech
Chepkurugat arap Chemusai
Kipkulei arap Bartai
Chepto arap Kipkech
Chepkonga arap Kitoto
Cheserem arap Kimoning
Kiplech arap Kipkech
Kiblesanfg arap Termus
Cheserem arap Lesil

Cherumben arap Kipterin replaced Cheserem arap Lesil who had resigned through government legal notice no. 329 of 29 April 1935. Through the same notice Chebaswonyi arap Kibaliat replaced Kiblesang arap Termus. Kiptoris arap Chepkochoi replaced Kipkoisir arap Kanda in 1936.

5. Government legal notice no. 197 of 7 March 1938

Nominated:
Busiendich arap Mursabit
Chepto arap Kech
Cheptiram arap Cheso
Kipkulei arap Bartai
Cheserem arap Kimoning
Chepkurgat arap Chemasai
Chemwerem arap Masingoi
Sero arap Cheso

Elected:

Cheserek arap Chesang
Kipkore arap Kitany
Chemelil arap Komen
Chelanga arap Kiborus
Chepkonga arap Kitoto
Chebi arap Bomonei
Chesire arap Kipkuto
Yego arap Mamandogi

On 30 June 1939 Chief Chemweno Kibor of Kibuswa was nominated into the council through an appeal by the DC Elgeyo-Marakwet to E. N. Hewitt, PC Nakuru, claiming that the chief was progressive and should not have to serve in land board with not as many deliberations as the council. Chemweno was fully incorporated in July 1939.

6. Government legal notice no. 516 of 31 May 1941

Nominated:
Sowe Kibiap, Marichor
Kite Tiren, Irong
Kigen Cheptum, Mutei
Chief Kipto Kisang, Sambirir
Kimuge Chemchor, Kapchemutwa

Elected:
Chief Busiendich Mursabit, Endo
Cheserek Kisang, Mokoro
Samalit Kipkech, Sambirir
Chemweno Chesir, Talai
Chelang'a Kiborus, Kibuswa
Kibos Kipsurgat, Cherangany
Kipkwen Cheresim, Sengwer
Chief Cheptiram Cheso, Kapchemutwa
Kipkulei Bartai, Irong
Chebi Bomonei, Mutei
Chelagat Baramao, Rokocho
Chesire Chepkuto, Maraichor
Chief Chemwerem Masingoi, Tumeyo

Yego Mamandogi, Metkei

Chief Kipsaina arap Kipkulei of Irong is nominated to the council through the government legal notice no. 705 of 8 August 1941. Kipkuto arap Chebi is nominated to the council as a representative of Mokoro on 25 November 1942. Kipsaina arap Kipkulei dies and is replaced by Chief Suter arap Kimeto on 19 January 1944.

7. Government legal notice no. ? of 7 March 1945

Nominated:
Kipto arap Kisang
Chemweno arap Chebor
Chepterit arap Chebi
Mikail Kiprop
Joshua Kibobei
Jacob Suter
Michael Bundotich
Joshua Cheptum
Kite arap Tiren
Chemwerem arap Masingoi

Elected:
Yego arap Mamandogi
Barmao arap Chebii
Chesire arap Ruto
Chelagat arap Barmao
Chebii arap Bomonei
Cherutich arap Tarei
Kimuge arap Chemchor
Samuel Koilege
Ruto arap Chebere
Chebi arap Chelanga
Kipto arap Chebet
Kipkiror arap Cheserek
Kiptalam arap Simbolei
Kipkwen arap Cheresim

Through government legal notice no. 980 of 9 October 1947 Elijah Chemweno replaced Joshua arap Cheptum who had resigned.

8. Government legal notice no. 192 of 20 February 1948

Nominated:
Chief Chemweno arap Chebor
Chief Michael Kiprop arap Cheptorus
Chief Kipto Kisang
Chief Yego arap Mamandogi
Michael Chelimo arap Bundotich
Joshua Isioi arap Chebobei
Chepterit arap Keture
Elijah arap Chemweno
Henry Ongoi arap Kibet
Kite arap Tiren

Elected:
Kilimo arap Cheserek
Kibowen arap Siter
Chebii arap Chelang'a
Ruto arap Cheberi
Cherutich arap Yano
Cheboi arap Chemitei
Kapcheptai arap Sirma
Edward Chelagat arap Chebor
Cherutich arap Tarei
Chepkurui arap Chepto
Bartilol arap Rotich
Kipto arap Chirchir
Chemworem arap Masingoi
Kipkaos arap Cherop

Six of the councillors were pronounced illiterate by an accompanying report. But it is hard to establish who is who among them.

On 25 May 1948 Chebiego arap Chebuluny replaces Cherutich arap Tarei who had retired. Through government notice no. 245 of 3 March 1950 Chepkiyeng arap Kibaror replaces Cherutich arap Yano who had retired and Cheserek arap Mariwot replaces Kibowen arap Suter who had also retired through government legal notice no. 575 of 20 May 1950.

9. Government legal notice no. 643 of 28 May 1948

Nominated:
Henry Ongoi arap Kibet, Cherangany
Lazaro arap Chepto, Kessup i.e. AIC
Lazaro arap Chumo, Nerkwo i.e. Roman Catholic
Sormwei arap Cheptum, Metkei
Chepterit arap Keture, Talai
Kite arap Terin, Irong
William arap Kimurgor
Chemweno arap Chebor
Kisang Kibor, Mokoro
Salim arap Chepkeitany, Mutei
Ayabei arap Koech, Tumeiyo

Elected:
Kipkiror arap Lasero, Endo
Kipkiror arap Kibor, Mokoro
Cherop arap Chebi, Sambirir
Daudi arap Kobuswa, Talai
Luka arap Kiptabus, Kibuswa
Cheboi arap Chemitei, Cherangany
Henry Ongoi arap Kibet, Cherangany
Kipchumba arap Lawich, Sengwer
Edward Chelagat arap Chepto, Kapchemutwa
Bartilol arap Rotich, Rokocho
Chebore arap Ruto, Tumeiyo
Kipto arap Komen, Metkei
Kipto arap Chirchir, Marichor
Chepkurui arap Chepto, Mutei
Chumo arap kandie, Lelan

There was an additional nomination in 1951 of Blasio Chebiego arap Kimona. Through government legal notice no. 866 of 18 May 1953 Cherutich arap Koigoch replaced Kipchumba arap Lawich who was convicted of a felony and was removed through government legal notice no. 237 of 1953.

10.   Government legal notice no. 1095 of 27 July 1954

Nominated:
Chief Chemweno arap Chebor, Kibuswa
Chief Salim Chelelgo arap Chepkaitany, Mutei
Chief Kipto arap Kisang, Sambirir
Chepterit arap Keture, Talai
Henry Ongoi arap Kibet, Cherangany
Kite arap Tiren, Irong
John Kotut arap Koitie, G. A. School
Chesang arap Kirorio, Mutei
Sormwei arap Cheptum, Metkei

Elected:
James arap Keitaba, Cherangany
Chumo arap kandie, Lelan
Kiboen arap Kimwasai, Sengwer
Kibiwot arap Cheboi, Sambirir
Edward arap Cheplagat, Kapchemutwa
Daudi arap Kapkabuswa, Talai
Luka arap Kiptabus, Kibuswa
Lazaro arap Chumo, Irong
Bartilol arap Rotich, Rokocho
Paulo arap Kipkoisir, Mutei
Kipto arap Chirchir, Marichor
Kipkiror arap Chemeitoi, Endo
William arap Cheraisi, Tumeyo
B. Kitum Kaino, Mokoro
Kipto arap Kimulwa, Metkei

Henry Ongoi resigned by not getting along with the chief. Edward Chelanga was convicted of cedar misappropriation in Shaw's Concession and was asked to defend himself against removal from the council. He wrote a letter dated 19 June 1956 to the PC through DC. It is not clear what happened thereafter. Chief Kisang Kirop replaced Henry Ongoi arap Kibet on 24 January 1957.

11. Government legal notice no. 2740 of 31 July 1957

Nominated:
Senior Chief Chemweno arap Chebor
Chief Willima Cherop arap Murgor
Chief Kiptoo arap Chirchir
Chief Kisang arap Kirop
Chief Cheboi arap Chemitei
Chepterit arap Keture
Kite arap Tiren
Chesang arap Kirorio
Kiprono arap Kibogy
Mirriam Chepto

Elected:
Salim Chelelgo arap Chepkaitany, Irong
Lazaro Ayabei arap Chumo
Edward Chelagat arap Chebet
Suter arap Chepkiyeng, Moiben
Joel Kibet arap Chebor
Josia Chemchor arap Katam, Soy
Cheboi arap Chepkenji, Soy
Chepkonga arap Maina, Mosop
James Cheptuigeny arap Ruto
Bernard Kaino arap Kitum, Endo
Kipkiror arap Chemeito, Endo
Kibiwot arap Cheboi, Sambirir
Kiptonui arap Rotich, Sengwer
Chepkurui arap Misto, Cherangany
Kimaget arap Surungai, Lelan

Ishmael Koimur (AIC School supervisor) from Marakwet was recommended to be incorporated into the council by DC on 10 October 1957 to balance Elgeyo numeric strength in the council. Cheserek arap Talai replaced Bernard Kaino arap Kitum who had resigned through government legal notice no. 2890 of 9 August 1958.

12. Government legal notice no. 1562 of 24 March 1960

Nominated:
Senior Chief Chemweno arap Chebor
Chief William Christpher Cherop arap Murgor
Chief Willie Kipto arap Chirchir
Chief Kisan arap Kirop
Chief Henry Ongoi arap Kibet
Chief Kibor arap Talai
Kite arap Tiren
Chepterit arap Keture
Edward Chelagat arap Kibogy
Miriam Chepto

Elected:
James Kiptuigeny arap Ruto
Chepkonga arap Maina
Cheboi arap Chepkenji
Rotich arap Muzee
Festo Lelit arap Kiplabul
Lazaro Aiyabei arap Chumo
Sila Kwambai arap Chepkultany
Joel Kibet arap Chebor
Isaiah Chebobei arap Alogin
Kiptonui arap Rotich
Kimeto arap Anwan
Kimaget arap Surungai
Bernard Kipkwony arap Bett
Cheserek arap Talai
Alexander Kirotich arap Chemeitoi

Four of the councillors Festo Lelit arap Kiplabul, Lazaro Aiyabei arap Chumo, Kimeto arap Anwan, and Bernard Kipkwony arap Bett were to be retired in 1962 according to the 13 March 1962 circular by the secretary to the council.

Cheserek arap Talai was disqualified on 7 August 1961 after being granted a nine-month sentence by the court at Tambach. He was replaced by Gabriel Kirop arap Chebet who was sworn in on 17 July 1961 at ADC Hall Tambach by DC J. A. Gardner. Arap Chebet was returned by majority votes on 12 May 1962. In addition, Miriam Chepto resigned and was replaced by Naomi Kipyab through government legal notice no. 4201 of 23 August 1961 together with Arap Chebet.

Resignations of Cheboi Chepkenji and Sila Kwambai arap Chepkultany were recognized through government legal notice no. 4699 of 12 October 1962 with the replacements of Zakayo Kipset arap Chebet and Martin Limo arap Kibaliat.

Several replacements were effected through Gazette notice 2691 of 12 June 1962: Lazaro Ayabei arap Chumo replaced Willie C. Cherop arap Murgor and Elijah Kiplelemet arap Chemweno replaced Wilie Kipto arap Chirchir in the first schedule; in the second schedule Mathew Kigen arap Komen replaced Festo Lelit arap Kiplabul, Henry Chepyator arap Chelimo replaced Lazaro Ayabei arap Chumo, and Chepkurui arap Kimisto replaced Kimeto arap Anwan, and Paulo Kilowin arap Chellewa replaced Bernard Kipkony arap Bett.

Kipchumba Foundation
P.O. Box 25380 – 00100 Nairobi, Kenya
www.kipchumbafound.org

www.ingramcontent.com/pod-product-compliance
Lightning Source LLC
Chambersburg PA
CBHW020606220526
45463CB00006B/2474